# Never Too Late

Joan E. Calliste

JOAN E. CALLISTE
PUBLICATIONS

ISBN: 978-1-966954-85-9 (paperback)
ISBN: 978-1-966954-84-2 (hardcover)
ISBN: 978-1-966954-86-6 (ebook)
Library of Congress Control Number: 2025921456

Printed in the United States of America

# Acknowledgement

I would like to dedicate this book to my three wonderful grandchildren, Jasmine, James and Francesca, with whom I love to spend time and do fun activities. I pray these lessons serve you well in life.

# Table of Contents

# A Father's Love

Mr. John is a proud father of three wonderful children- two boys and a girl. They were doing well in school and were involved in sports, church and in various community activities. Everyone loves them in their neighborhood as they were the children any parent would wish to have.

Every evening after school, they all did their homework and would even tutor their friends who needed help in Math. When homework was done, they were off to practice football, and then to music lessons. Mr. John was well-respected by his two boys and they came to him for counsel often. He advised them to work hard in school and make their parents proud.

All was well until one afternoon, when Mr. John received a call from his daughter's teacher: Alice skipped school. At first, Mr. John thought it hard to believe. Then, two weeks later, he received another call with news that Alice was seen joyriding with her friends. Still, Mr. John was not convinced- every evening, Alice came home in her school uniform. What he did not realize was that Alice carried a change of clothing in her bag every day. The next morning, Mr. John noticed Alice wearing casual clothes. "Where is your uniform?" asked Mr. John. Alice did not answer.

It was then that Mr. John informed his wife of what was going on with Alice. Alice's mom was shocked to hear that their daughter was engaging in such reckless behavior. She became worried, but Mr. John assured his wife that he would handle the matter.

One night, Mr. John called Alice to have a talk. He asked her what was going on with school. Immediately, Alice hung her head in silence, and tears streamed down her face. Mr. John said, "Alice, you know that you can talk to me. I'm here to help you." Still, Alice was not ready to open up.

The next day, Mr. John took the family to their favorite mall. While Mom and the boys went shopping for shoes, Dad and Alice sat in a quiet spot. He hugged Alice and said, "Alice, I love you. But lately, you've been heading down the wrong path. Please tell me what's wrong. My job is to protect my family- when one of us is hurting, we all feel the pain." Alice apologized to her dad and explained that she and her friends were being bullied at school. "We just didn't feel safe at school. I felt trapped."

Mr. John assured Alice that he would handle the matter with her school teacher right away, and Alice promised never to skip school again. As the family drove home from the mall, Mr. John and his wife had a talk with their kids about feelings. The kids agreed to talk to their parents whenever something was troubling them, instead of keeping it inside. The day ended in a big family group hug, and Alice shouted, "I love you, Dad! You're the best."

# The Invitation

A family that never believed in religion was once invited by their neighbor to a prayer meeting. The parents didn't attend, but their nine-year-old daughter, Lizzie, decided to go. The neighbor picked Lizzie up and took her to the meeting.

Lizzie enjoyed the prayer service and promised to attend again. The neighbor told Lizzie to be ready at 9 a.m. on Saturday morning. Lizzie was excited to go and learn about Jesus, but when her dad found out that the neighbor was a Seventh-day Adventist, he became very angry. He banned Lizzie from going to the neighbor's church and stated that she would be punished if she disobeyed.

Lizzie cried; she wanted to learn more about Jesus. On Saturday morning, as soon as her dad left for work, she went to church with the neighbor. Sure enough, dad punished Lizzie when he found out. However, punishment or no punishment, Lizzie decided that she had to go to church- she wanted to learn more about Jesus. She loved the singing, the Bible verses, and the prayers she learned to say. From that day on, Lizzie prayed to Jesus and asked, "Please, Jesus, help my dad to stop punishing me for going to church. Help him come and learn about You too."

One night, Lizzie's mom overheard her prayer. She decided to go to church with Lizzie to see what was going on. As mom got ready for church the next Saturday morning, Lizzie's brother decided to go with them too. When Dad discovered that his family went to church, he became very upset and withdrawn; he did not speak to anyone for two days. Then, Lizzie's mom told him, "You should come to church with us and see what your daughter has been enjoying these past few weeks."

"Never," replied Lizzie's dad. In time, Lizzie's mom came to know and love Jesus, and began to pray for her husband. "Please let him say yes and come, just this once."

Sure enough, the next time Lizzie's mom asked, Dad agreed to come to church with them. That Sabbath morning, the Pastor preached a sermon that seemed to be just what the family needed to hear. The message was about faith and how to trust in the Lord. As they listened, Lizzie held her dad's hand and began praying silently.

The Lord answered Lizzie's silent prayer; six months later, her entire family accepted Jesus. It was such a joyful moment. The family began praying together and continued to attend church together. Dad apologized to Jesus and to Lizzie for the times he punished her for attending church. Lizzie forgave her dad, and she thanked her neighbor for inviting them to church all those months ago. The family continued to serve and praise the Lord.

Indeed, nothing is impossible with God.

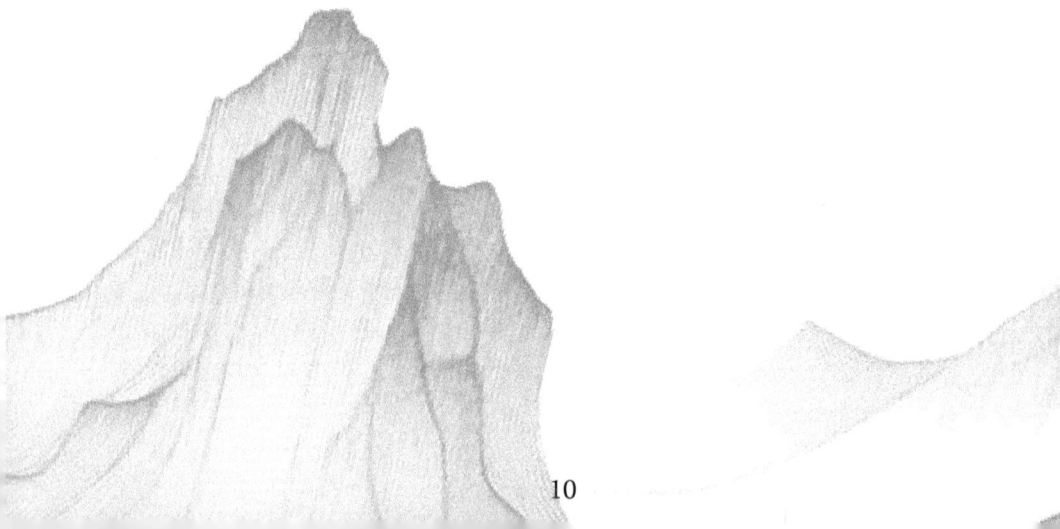

# Standing Together

**M**any years ago, a group of students attended a school bazaar. The purpose of the event was to raise money for charity. Sales booths offering delicious food, snacks, ice cream, and much more were on display across the school grounds. Talent shows were held ,and children modeled fantastic clothing. The day was full of laughter and fun.

At one point during the event, the group of students engaged in biblical discussions. One of the topics was the Ten Commandments, and a debate ensued on whether or not Christians had to keep all of the laws listed there. Some thought that one could worship any day of the week; others thought that as long as you pray, there's nothing wrong with telling the occasional white lie.

The discussion continued until one of the students decided to take some of the money she had raised from her sales booth. The cashier at the booth saw this and stated, "Wait! We have to count all the money!" The student taking the money replied, "It's okay! If we can worship any day of the week, then that means we can steal, too!"

After returning the money to its proper place, the student explained that all the laws hold equal weight, and breaking one is to break them all. She then explained that the laws of God stand forever, and are the same for us as they were for the people who lived in Bible times.

The charity event turned out to be a great success, and the group of students all learned that all of God's laws are true and for their own benefit. Many students who'd never learned to keep the Sabbath began doing so, and found it to be a very rewarding commandment to follow.

# Friends Forever

Merry and Brady made plans to become business partners in the car trading business. They started with used cars, and as time went by, business began to grow. One summer morning, they decided to sell cold beverages out of their garage – a venture that also became successful. As Merry and Brady worked together, their friendship grew stronger. They were open and honest with each other in all their dealings.

After paying for the startup business expenses in the first few months, they decided to split the profit from the monthly garage. Five years into the business, however, Brady became ill. He asked Merry to be the beneficiary of his portion of profits should he pass away. Unfortunately, Merry thought to take this opportunity to steal from the business and take more than his fair share.

Little did Merry know that Brady would make a full recovery. After six months, Brady returned to work and began asking questions about the books. When Merry could not give an account for the discrepancies, he confessed to his friend what he had been doing. Disappointed, Brady requested his share of the startup money, as well as his share of the profits from the past six months. Merry apologized, regretful that he let his greed get the better of him. Brady forgave Merry, and the two decided to put their business finances in the hands of an external accountant. They remained in business together – but more importantly, they remained friends. They chose to never again allow money - or anything else - get in the way of their friendship.

# Do You Know My Father?

L eo was a loving, caring little fellow who always looked out for others. He tried to make people smile in any way he could, and encouraged them when the y were feeling down. He would tell his friends to never give up, reminding them that whatever problem they faced, God was able to fix it.

Leo loved sports;  and his favorite of all was football. One evening while playing, Leo took a fall and hurt himself. The accident left him with a permanent limp and a lifelong disability. Nonetheless, Leo refused to feel sorry for himself. He believed that God was able to make the impossible possible, and that He could turn his situation around for good. He chose to move forward with his life.

A few weeks after Leo's accident, his community planned to put on a Sports Day event. Jokingly, Leo's friends dared him to take part in the running event. Leo asked the event coordinator,

"What's the distance?" "Four laps around the park," replied the coordinator. "No, you can't do that!" said one of Leo's friends. "You won't be able to run that far." Leo laughed and said, "Do you know who my father is? The God of universe is able! I can't do it in my own strength, but with God I can."

Sports Day arrived, and ten people entered the running contest. They all gathered at the starting point. When the whistle blew, each one took off. By the end of the third lap, Leo was in last place. His friends laughed at him from the sidelines.

"We knew you couldn't do it," one of them said. "Watch me now!" Leo thought to himself.

Then, the unexplainable happened - Leo passed seven people and came in at third place! His friends were shocked and excited. They rushed to Leo after the race, asking him how he did it.

Leo replied, "The God of the impossible was in control. He is my Father!"

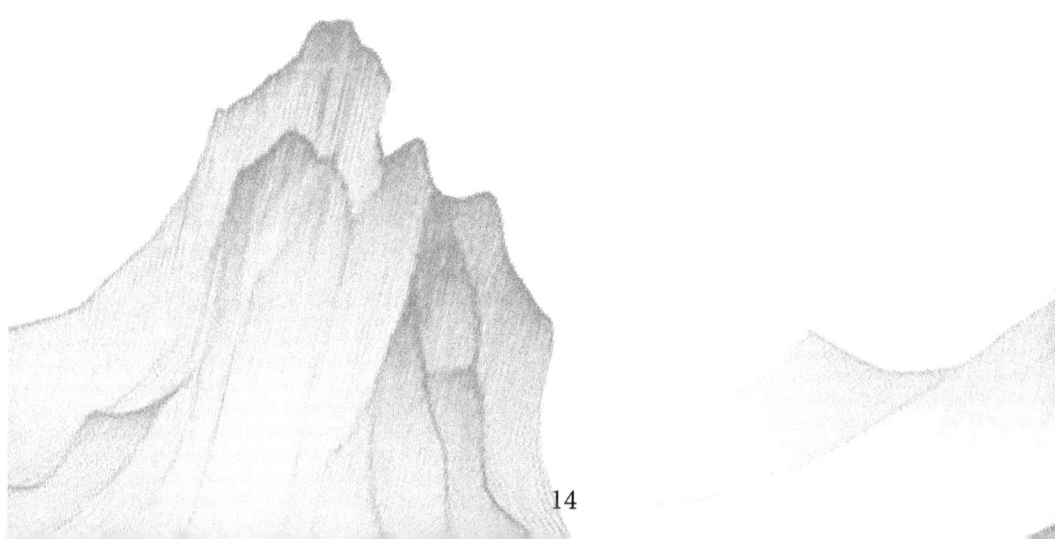

# A Simple Farmer

A wealthy professor once had a conversation with someone he assumed   was a businessman. The professor thought he could deceive the man by pretending to be interested in a business partnership. Without even giving the man a chance to say his name, the professor approached the gentleman and began proposing a partnership. After listening to the professor's proposition, the gentleman smiled and asked,

"May I introduce myself? I'm Mr. Walker."

"Oh, I'm sorry, "I'm Professor Johnson. Can we meet for drinks later at the Peterman's Pub?"

Mr. Walker agreed, and the two later enjoyed each other's company at the pub. Their conversation went well; however, Professor Johnson was shocked to discover that Mr. Walker was a simple farmer and not a wealthy businessman.

"Sir, no disrespect- but may I ask, do you have a family to support?" asked Professor Johnson.

"Yes," replied Mr. Walker. Knowing where the professor's questions would lead, Mr. Walker continued,

"You see, we have learned to be happy with what we have. We live a decent life- my kids attend private school, we own our home, and we do fun things together as a family. Wealth doesn't always make you happy. You must be disciplined with your finances and control your spending, so that you're not always wanting more and more."

That night, Professor Johnson left the pub both astonished and troubled. He was a wealthy man with a lavish lifestyle- yet he did not own a home, and his kids attended public school. They wore brand-name clothing and shoes, and his wife only carried designer handbags.

He realized that he'd been investing in the wrong things, and this way of living caused him sleepless nights. Despite his luxurious lifestyle, the professor was deeply unhappy. Professor Johnson began to understand the value of simple living. After all, in the end, one can't take their riches to the grave.

# The Community Concert

Mr. Lloyd decided to host a concert. However, there were no professional performers in the community. To spread the word and find local talent, Mr. Lloyd drove around in his car and, using an external loudspeaker, made the announcement as he passed from street to street.

Anyone interested in performing could come to his office and show their talent. He welcomed all kinds of talents- singing, acting, comedy/talk show hosting, and more. Not everyone in the community agreed that opening participation to everyone was a good idea, but Mr. Lloyd continued with the plans.

On the day of the concert, community members packed the stadium. Everyone enjoyed the talents that were showcased. Each performer received loud applause - and even some gifts of encouragement.

There was one performer in particular, however, who stood out for an unusual act: He was speaking to a person who wasn't there. His name was Andy. Andy then started making faces, and, out of nowhere, shouted:

"I have overcome my fears! Now I can stand fearlessly in public! Thank you, Mr. Lloyd, for allowing me this opportunity instead of turning me away. With my make-believe talent, at least I can make people laugh!"

The crowd applauded loudly for the boy. After the concert, new opportunities within the community opened up for him, and he went on to help other kids overcome their fears as well.

We all have fears at some point in life. Just like Andy, we too can overcome them. We must believe in ourselves and replace fear with faith.

# Payments: Cheque Only

Mr. Parker owed the bank some money that he had borrowed to purchase a home. The agreement was that payments were to be made to the bank by cheque; but Mr. Parker decided to pay in cash. He figured that as long as he made his payments on time, it wouldn't matter how he paid.

Mr. Parker went to the loan manager with his cash. To his surprise, the loan manager refused to accept it. He reminded Mr. Parker of their agreement : payment was to be made by cheque only.

"Does it really matter how I pay?" asked Mr. Parker. "As long as I pay my debt, their shouldn't be an issue, right?"

The manager firmly replied that he would only accept cheque. Mr. Parker became very angry. But then, upon reflection, he heard a voice saying, "Disobedience results in pain."

Mr. Parker went home and reflected some more. As he searched in the Bible, he realized that he was guilty of disobedience and of breaking God's laws- not just in this instance, but throughout his life.

Mr. Parker went back to the loan manager to ask for forgiveness and it was accepted. He then sought forgiveness from his friends whom he'd hurt in the past, and even apologized to his parents, to whom he had been very disrespectful as a child. He said to them:

"I'm very sorry for the pain I caused you both. Please forgive me. Looking back, I know it was not easy, and I thank God that you never gave up on me. I love you."

Faithful, enduring love sustained Mr. Parker and eventually led him to accept Jesus. In the end, love is the key to true success in life.

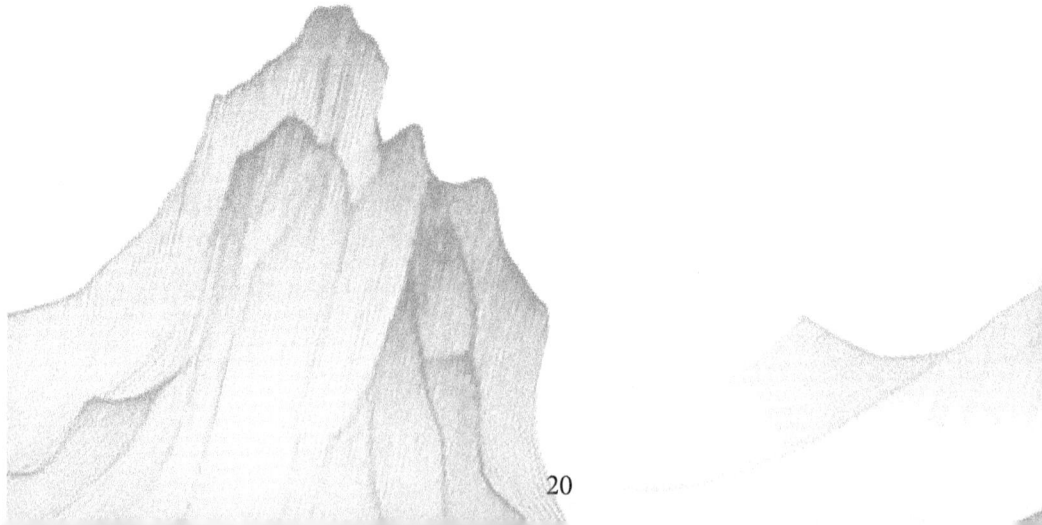

# Faith In Action

Jannett attended public school all her life. After graduating from high school, she wanted to attend a Christian college. Unfortunately, Jannett's parents couldn't afford the cost of a private college, and she ended up going to a public college instead.

Jannett wasn't happy at her school. One day, while talking to her friend Nancy, Jannett mentioned that she wanted to attend a Christian college but couldn't afford it.

Nancy smiled for a moment, then asked, "Do you believe in prayers?" "Yes," Jannette replied.

"Then let's pray that the Lord will make a way and grant your heart's desire," said Nancy. "Nothing is impossible with Him."

At the end of Jannett's second semester, she received an invitation to attend Smith's Christian College. The letter stated that she would have to take a placement test in order to qualify for a full academic scholarship as only the top 5 students would receive the award. Not knowing whether she would make it or not, she shouted, "Thank you God!" She called her parents and told them the good news - that God had answered her prayers.

Before her exam, Jannett and Nancy decided to spend extra time in prayer. Two weeks later, the results came out: Jannett placed third! She was so thankful that God granted her heart's desire. She also thanked Nancy for encouraging her to keep hope alive. From that day forward, both girls had a powerful testimony of the goodness of God.

# Tough Love

The Lewis family was a happy, outgoing bunch. The Lewise's had two children, Laura and Peter. The children would receive discipline whenever they disobeyed their parents, but their friends were not. One day Peter asked his dad,

"Why do you punish us for the wrong things we do, while our friends aren't punished at all?"

"Because I love you both," Dad explained. "It is my job to teach you wrong from right, and to keep you out of trouble."

"So are you saying that my friends' parents don't care?" asked Peter.

"No, son," Dad replied. "Other families have different ways of disciplining their children. Don't compare us to them; each parent is responsible for their own home."

"I love you and your sister so much," Dad continued. "It would break my heart to see either of you go down the wrong path in life and, God forbid, end up in the hands of the police. This is why you must be disciplined in love at all times. I want both of you to be a good example to others in your community, and to make wise choices that will help you succeed in life."

Tough love pays off.

# The River Rescue

It was a hot summer day. Betty and Joyce decided to cool off from the heat by heading to the river for a swim. They were having so much fun, and as time went by, more people came to join them. The group climbed on rocks and played together in the water.

Soon, the area became very crowded. Betty and Joyce decided to have a break and have some snacks. They laid out on their towels in a cool, shaded spot. They began to reminisce on good times they had in the past. Some people from the group began playing football, and the girls asked if they could join them. Everyone was enjoying the game and having a good time, when someone kicked the ball into the river.

As Betty and Joyce watched the ball sail out into the deep, they saw someone jump in after it. Betty recognized the person as Tommy, a boy who had been very mean to her some time ago. Tommy was struggling to stay afloat in the rapidly moving water. "Yes," thought Betty. "This is payback."

Then, as she stood watching Tommy drift farther into the deep, tears began to stream down Betty's face. She prayed, "Lord, help me," and jumped in to save him. She swam toward Tommy, grabbed him, and pulled him to safety. When Tommy was able to catch his breath, he exclaimed, "Thank you so much."

As he recovered, he spoke softly. "Of all people, I never expected you to help me. I'm sorry for my foolish ways in the past. Your kindness today has shown me the importance and power of forgiveness."

# The Stranger

Two friends, Terrence and Roger, went hiking on a bright summer's day. Everything was going well on their journey through the woods. They came upon a waterfall and had a refreshing drink of water. After resting for a while, they decided to hike in different directions and meet back at the waterfall at the end of the day. They would then open up their tent, camp for the night, and continue hiking the next morning until it was time to head home.

Around midday, before the two friends had the chance to split off, they heard someone crying out for help in the distance. The weather suddenly changed, and it began to rain. Terrence was hesitant to go out in the rain and help the person calling out, but Roger persuaded him, and the two began searching. Soon, they found a man lying down by an old treehouse- he had broken his ankle. The two friends bandaged the stranger's foot with a strip of cloth and got a stick to help him walk. Together, they guided him to safety and called for help.

The friends were able to contact one of the stranger's family members, who soon came to the rescue. As they arrived to transport their relative, they offered to give Roger and Terrence a ride as well. The two friends agreed and were grateful for the ride.

As they were loading their things into the car, Roger realized that he had forgotten his wallet at home- they had no money to travel back. Were it not for the kindness of strangers, they would not have been able to get home. That day, the two friends were reminded that the good one does for others comes right back around to them.

# No Work, No Pay

A young man named Larry was looking for work. He met another young man, Bobby, who was also looking for a job. Neither of them had a special career; they were handymen trying to earn money.

The two went to a warehouse seeking employment. The foreman interviewed both of them with just a few, simple questions. He then decided to employ Bobby, and told Larry to return in two weeks.

On his way home, Larry stopped at a bakery and asked if there was work available. He was told to come the next morning at 7:45 am. Larry was happy and thought that working in a bakery would be much easier than working in the warehouse.

Larry arrived at the bakery the next morning, ready to start his new job. For the first two weeks, Larry's employer was very impressed with his performance. Although Larry wasn't particularly interested in the work, Larry knew that it was his only way to get money. After a while, Larry thought to himself, "I'll just find a quiet place to hide out every now and again during work hours." His plan went well the first few times - until one rainy day when the boss, Mr. Uriah, came into the bakery looking for Larry. Larry was nowhere to be found.

"He thinks I'm working but I'm not, he thinks I'm working but I'm not!"

Mr. Uriah just shook his head and returned to the bakery. Instead of confronting Larry about his negligence, Mr. Uriah decided to teach him a lesson. Come payday, Larry would receive the surprise of his life. Mr. Uriah sang to himself,

"Larry thinks I'm paying, but I'm not!"

On Friday evening, Larry went to the boss's office to receive his pay. The door was closed, and he could hear Mr. Uriah humming from inside. Larry knocked on the door, and the boss replied in song:

"You think I'm paying, but I'm not! When I thought you were working, you were not! It's simple: no work, no pay."

Larry pleaded with his boss and apologized, promising to never neglect his work again. He was able to keep his job - but did not receive any pay for that week. Larry learned his lesson the hard way.

From that day on, he worked earnestly- even putting in overtime- as he knew that Mr. Uriah was not one to joke around. Larry shared his experience with other young men and warned them not to make the same mistakes.

Hard work pays.

# Love is in the Air

O ne Sunday evening as I strolled through Riverdale Park, the weather was nice, cool, and very breezy. As I walked further into the park, I came across a bench. I decided to sit for a while and enjoy the quiet moment. People were walking by, children were bike riding, and birds were singing sweetly in the trees.

The song of one of the birds caught my attention. It sounded as if it were saying, "Love is in the air." I called the attention of a lady passing by to ask her opinion. She paused and listened carefully, then thought for a moment and said, "Maybe the bird is saying that very phrase-just in its own language." The human mind could interpret the bird's song as saying, "Enjoy creation! Smell the fresh air, enjoy good friendship, and, most of all, sense that love is in the air."

Out of love for mankind, the Creator made a beautiful world. If we embrace love more and more, the heartaches we carry will be overridden by the power of love.

I challenge you to choose love. It will open doors in high places. You will experience an inner peace whose effect is greater than that of any medicine. When others notice the spark in your eyes and are drawn to you, smile and tell them, "Love is the answer."

Sometimes, my friend, all it takes is genuine love.

# The Contagious Smile

Every morning for a year, I walked past the same fire station at around 6:30 a.m. on my way to the gym. I never paid attention to the people I passed there; I hardly ever said good morning. Most of the time, I just smiled and went along my way.

One morning, as I was approaching the station, I noticed something fall in front of me. It was a banana peel that someone from the fire station had thrown out. I shook my head, smiled, and continued along my way. As I walked past the fire station, the same individual shouted some unpleasant remarks to me. This time, I waved to them and smiled, then kept going.

I later found out that the individual's name was Maldo, and he was intentionally trying to upset me- he wanted to change my smile into anger. Disappointed that I was still smiling, he approached me two weeks later and asked, "What will it take to stop your beautiful smile?"

I looked him in the eye and said, "To smile is easier than to frown!"

A smile says a million words. In the middle of a storm, in the moments you cannot speak, you learn to smile. You learn that a frown stirs up anger, which is detrimental to your health.

By the end of the conversation, the entire fire unit had a better perspective, and their community became friendlier because of my smiles. Smiling is contagious, and it helps keep your stress levels under control. It is a priceless gift that you can give to brighten someone's day.

This story is dedicated to my wonderful granddaughter, Jasmine E. Coombs, who is always smiling.

# Magic Words Matter

Have you ever stopped to think about the power of words? They can make or break a friendship. Growing up, words had no special meaning to me - in my culture, you just talked, because freedom of speech was your right. Today, however, we are living in an age in which we must be attentive to our words.

When others are helpful to us, simple words like "please," "excuse me," and "thank you" can save us from difficulties. Allow me to share an example from my past experience:

I was traveling to an unfamiliar town. I had directions, but was still unsure if I was going the right way. Hot, thirsty, and tired of walking back and forth, I decided to ask someone for help. I walked up to a gentleman standing by a bus stop and asked:

"Can you tell me which way I should go to get to Bridge Port Road?" He looked at me, then walked away.

I began to feel a sense of dejection when my inner voice reminded me, "Use the magic words! You should have said, 'Good afternoon,' or 'Excuse me-' and then asked your question!'"

I turned in the opposite direction and, sure enough, the same gentleman was standing there.

I was running late, and my time was short. Swallowing my pride, I approached him again- this time in a more respectful manner. I gently asked for directions, and the man told me to walk to my right-hand side and pass Rose Avenue, after which I would see Bridge Port Road.

Smiling, I loudly replied, "Thank you, sir! I appreciate your help."

Finally, I reached my destination.

We must take time to be thoughtful, courteous, and compassionate. Avoid hostility towards others. As the scripture says, "Kind words turn away wrath, but grievous words stir up anger."

# The Light of Life

Let's talk about light and darkness- not the light you turn off with a switch in a dark room, but the light that shines from the choices we make in our lives.

When we make bad choices- cheating, stealing, making fun of others, and so on - the trouble we find ourselves in becomes the darkness in our lives. We can overcome this darkness by following a path that would make our light shine. Helpfulness, honesty, and kindness- these are qualities that our friends, family and the people around us can see as evidence of the light within us. These qualities prove us to be light-bearers in this world.

We can find examples of others who made good choices from the Bible, from Daniel, who purposed in his heart to refrain from eating the King's delicious (but unhealthy) food, to Dorcas, a seamstress who made clothing for those in need. These are examples to follow, as the choices we make determine our destiny.

We must stand up for what is right and others are going to look up at us, all it takes is obedience and self-control. Keep in mind that we are the leaders of tomorrow. Just like light that shines through the darkness, our choices can make a difference.

# My Treasure Chest

Treasures are the things that are most important to us - personal files, monetary savings, family pictures, and things we hold onto in case of emergencies.

Many of us have that special someone that we trust - someone with whom we discuss our deepest secrets - our treasures.

If I were to share with you what my treasure is, would you want to be my beneficiary? You would be surprised to know that my treasure is not one of monetary value- it is not an insurance policy or checking account. In fact, my treasure is not of worldly gain. It may seem strange when I let you in on what it is....

The moment of truth: here is my priceless treasure - my heartfelt thanks for life, peace of mind, good health, and the love of family and friends.

In these difficult times there is still hope- if we focus on how we can make a difference in our families, friendships and communities. You see, friends, while money is something we need, it takes more than money to make us happy. It is the priceless things- love, kindness, compassion, teaching our children to be caring- that I keep in my treasure chest.

When I walk by, others feel my presence and sense a joy that makes them smile. A simple, friendly "hello" can cheer a broken heart. This is my treasure - making a difference in the lives of others is my purpose.

# The Message

This message is to guide a generation preparing to face the real world. First, allow the Lord to be the center of your life. We are living in crucial times, and it takes divine intervention to lead us to the right path.

Next, get an education, and find your purpose in life as this will help you shape your future. Whatever career path you choose, be sure to have an additional skill or trade under your belt in case things do not go as planned as life is full of unexpected obstacles.

Don't be fooled-life is more than partying and having fun. Nothing is wrong with enjoying yourself occasionally, but that must not become your driving motivation.

Be a leader. Set high standards that will take you through life's journey. Believe in yourself. Maintain a positive attitude. Respect yourself and respect others.

I know that there are times when you think that the older folks don't listen to you but there is no need to divide us. All we want is for you to be successful in life. Sure enough, you all are the leaders of tomorrow.

Now is the time to start exhibiting the kind of leadership your community will expect from you in the near future. They are looking for leaders who will be caring and sympathetic-leaders who will listen to their concerns and go the extra mile to help those who have real needs and require special attention. They are looking for a patient leader - prudent in both words and in deed.

# Your Choice

Isn't it interesting that you are born into the world with no knowledge of how you are cared for? Rather, you grow into knowing wonderful parents who cared for and continue to care for you.

Knowing where you've come from, please be thankful. Get a good education, stay in school, think big, set goals and always have a backup plan.

Making some hard choices may open doors of opportunity. Challenge yourself and see the great wonders you can accomplish. Others will look up to you and see an example of leadership – one that can guide them to a brighter future. Indeed, our actions can make a difference in the lives of others.

It brought tears to my eyes when a young man shared his life experience with me; he had dropped out of school and was living on the streets.

One late evening, he was sitting in an old car by the side of the road. A man call out to him and asked why he is not at home. The young man hung his head and said, "Sir, I have no home."

The man had a surprised look on his face. He then asked, "What is your name?"

"Johnny," the young man said.

The man then introduced himself. "I am Mr. Russell. Let me share something about myself with you."

"In life, I've come across many obstacles- but I did not give up. You deserve better, and I'm sure you desire change for yourself. I can help you if you are willing."

Mr. Russell had made some hard choices in life, and his experience allowed him the empathy and wisdom to help out young Johnny. He took him in as a son and cared for him.

Johnny went back to school and did very well, graduating with high honors. Today, thanks to Mr. Russell, he is a guidance counselor with a bright future. He learned the importance of education the hard way, but now has a wonderful story to share – one that inspires and encourages others.

You can be a mentor to others and make a difference. Life will be more meaningful when you choose a path that considers the well-being of others.

# The Inner Voice

The fact is, I was born into a poor family. At times I didn't know where my next meal was coming from. People call me out of my name and looked down on me.

But when it seems as if your world is hopelessly crashing down, know that it's not!

During those days I thought to myself, "There has to be a better way of life."

Then, one morning, it was as if I felt a touch on my shoulder, and a voice whispered,

"You deserve better."

At that moment, I knew I had to stop pitying myself. The choice was mine:
where do I go from here?

I did not have much to start with. I got a job in a little tea shop - the salary was meagre, but it was better than none.

For whatever reason, the customers appreciated my services. After about five months, Mrs. Buddy, one of the customers, offered me a job at her garment store. I hesitated at first, but she assured me that my lack of experience would not be a problem. The following month I went to work for her, and the salary was much better! I could now finally start saving some money.

After a week on the job, I was surprised to discover that the garment store and the tea shop had the same owner.

Mrs. Buddy explained that from the first day she saw me on the job at the tea shop, she thought that I would be a good worker for her garment store.

Now, my life is moving in a better direction. I went from a pauper to a store manager, and I now realize that the choices I make are what will take me to my destiny.

Never give up. Believe that you can be whoever you want to be. Have confidence in yourself, and opportunities will open doors in high places for you.

# Transit Dilemma

One busy Monday morning on my way to work, I stood waiting at the bus stop with my friend Carol. I noticed buses passing by our stop, each one reading, "Next Bus Please." After about half an hour, Carol decided to walk to the train station and see if the trains would get us there faster.

When she arrived, the train conductors were on break. She asked, "How long before the train leaves?"

The train dispatcher said it would be another fifteen minutes. While waiting, however, she heard an announcement saying that the train was out of service. Upset, she stormed back to the bus stop.

"What happened?" I asked her.

"Can you believe that the train is also out of service? How am I going to get to work?" she said.

At this point, my determination kicked in - and I couldn't care less. The next bus that came by- in-service or not - I was getting on.

I stopped the next bus. The driver gently opened the door to inform me, "This bus is out of service."

I got on anyway. The driver continued to repeat himself, "Ma'am, this bus is going to the yard." Sure enough, the bus arrived at the yard.

When the driver saw how determined I was to get to work, he looked at me and said, "Mama, you are amazing. If everyone showed such determination, this world would be a better place. I have no choice but to take you to your destination."

He took me where I needed to go, and I thanked him, saying, "Have a wonderful day, Sir!"

# Replacing Anger with Kindness

Have you ever thought about the future obstacles you may have to overcome in order to be successful?

I once worked in a law firm as a secretary. My responsibility was to keep the files organized and up to date. Because of my loyalty, I was offered a promotion. I was excited to move up to higher heights! However, for some unknown reason, it was given to someone else. I was upset, but did not hold any grudges.

I continued to do my job faithfully. I was reminded that in life we face many obstacles - but moving on from them affords us even greater opportunities.

About a month later, the individual who had been chosen for the promotion approached me and asked for help him with some paperwork that he didn't understand.

Can you imagine what went through my mind?

I was silent for a moment. "This is my opportunity to make a difference," I thought. I replaced my anger with kindness. It was not easy, but I learned to smile - knowing that love overcomes anger and opens doors in high places.

Eventually, 1 was promoted.

# Living with Purpose

We are living in troublesome times. We must stay focused and keep our lives' purpose at the forefront of our thoughts.

The decisions you make will carry you through a lifetime. Tomorrow is never guaranteed - you may have to change careers, or even re-evaluate some friendships. Life, therefore, has many ups and downs.

You can weather the storms of life if you listen to your heart. Believe in yourself, and you will find that your issues aren't as overwhelming as you think. I have heard of others who hit rock bottom, but because they had a plan in place, they were able to survive and come back stronger than before.

You can learn from your mistakes. You can override your issues and emerge victorious.

We all should have a purpose for our lives. By living with purpose, you may inspire someone else to believe in themselves - to know that in life's worst moments, there is still hope. We all deal with our struggles in different ways, but we can all come out victoriously at the end of the day. Let's be compassionate towards those we see struggling and drowning in their troubles. Lend a helping hand- not out of judgment, but out of genuine love.

# The Uncertainty of Life: Effects of COVID 19

In 2020, we were faced with a deadly disease for which there is still no real cure. Life seemed helpless; people were scared. Never in my wildest dreams did I imagine that life could take such a drastic change.

Where do we go from here? This is not a dream - lives have truly been shattered. Life after the pandemic will never be the same.

Change is hard to accept yet now, we must pick up the pieces as best as we can. We must help each other in whatever ways we can. Befriend others. Learn to love the unlovable. In these difficult times, even the simple act of making someone smile will help to keep their stress level down.

We cannot allow the effects of COVID-19 to destroy us completely.

Some of us have lost loved ones, and we have experienced a lot of pain. Family and friends - keep checking on each other. We can never heal in isolation. Most of all, we need the strength of our Heavenly Father to carry us through these challenging times.

We cannot forget to thank our frontline workers from the bottom of our hearts. Visit those who are in need. Say a prayer for them. Letting them know we care will brighten up their day.

It doesn't take much - simply listening, making someone laugh, bringing them flowers- these little things can save someone a doctor's visit caused by stress and anxiety.

COVID-19, we refuse to let you destroy us completely.

# The Year 1974

In April of 1974, my family experienced a great tragedy. One of my brothers was involved in a serious motorcycle accident. The doctors told us to be strong, because the outcome did not look good. We were crushed - the pain was unbearable.

Our pastor came and prayed with the family. He then said to my mom, "Pray for a miracle from the Lord; pray for restoration and hope." We cried and prayed, asking the Lord to revive our hope.

Then one Sunday evening, as I was on my way to visit him, a heartbreaking thought came to me. "What if we have to make funeral arrangements for his twenty- first birthday?"

"No!" I cried aloud.

At that moment, I became helpless - no human comfort could cheer me up. Then I heard the Savior whisper,

"Come, my child."

After years of running, in my darkest hour, I had a personal encounter with Jesus.

I answered "Yes, Lord," and He assured me that my brother wouldn't die. Saying yes to Jesus was the best decision I ever made. My life now has meaning, and I thank the Lord for never giving up on me.

There are times I fall, and each time, He is there to rescue me. I had the joy of seeing that same brother get married. Later on, I saw the hand of the Lord save my daughter when she excitedly ran in front of a car to greet her favorite uncle on his wedding day.

Friends, Jesus is the way of life and our only source of hope. Let him lead you – starting today.

# Precious Memories

**G**randparents are very important in the lives of their grandchildren. If you have them in your life, cherish every moment you have with them.

For various reasons, not all grandparents have the opportunity to spend time with their grandchildren. Thinking back to my own experience, I realize we were very lucky to have our grandparents in our lives. My grandpa was especially present; he would play his guitar and sing songs for us.

Christmas time, was particularly fun. He would say to us, "Let us go parang (Trinidadian Christmas celebration with music, dance and food)!" We did not know the songs, but there were always lots of goodies to eat and drink.

Sadly, grandpa passed away many years ago. To this day, we still miss him.

Grandma was a great cook and a wonderful baker; we have so many fun memories with her. We would go shopping, walk long distances, and sometimes spend the day down by the river - washing and swimming. Suddenly, you would hear the bells on the bike of the snow cone man, and we would race as kids to see who would reach him first.

There were times when grandma spoiled us by letting us have our way. At times she'd even give us money to buy whatever we wanted. That said, when she got serious, you had to be on your best behavior- you wouldn't like the consequences if you weren't.

Nevertheless, days with grandma were indeed happy days. When she died, our family was heartbroken, but we now have a lifetime of precious memories. We thank the Lord for keeping us to this day while she sleeps in peace.

# The Teenage Years

My teenage years were happy times. I lived in a small community where everyone knew each other. The people were very friendly.

Sometimes we would get into mischief as teenagers, which was lots of fun. We would raid our neighbors' fruit trees, and when they came out of their houses we would dash into the bushes and roll down the hill into the river- whatever we could think of that would make us laugh.

Sometimes, under a bright moonlight night, we would all come together and play games like hide and seek, jump rope, and "Who Stole the Cookie from the Cookie Jar?"

When it was time to do our chores, we would help each other out to get the job done faster. There were no stand pipe near our homes, so we had to go by the stand pipe a mile away to fetch water. With teamwork, we got the job done.

On the weekends, we would make bread. One of our friends had a big mud oven that could hold about eight loaves at a time. We had to gather bundles of wood to light the oven, which took about an hour to heat up. Then we'd take out the charcoal and put the bread to bake.

Those were the most delicious loaves of bread. When eaten hot with butter and a cup of hot chocolate. They created lasting lasting memories we cherish until today.

Sometimes I stroll down memory lane and think back to those times... they were happy, fun days.

# Never Too Late

Throughout my lifetime, I have had many opportunities. Some I embraced, and they worked out well for a time. Others I just allowed to pass me by-often because I felt I was not capable of doing certain things, and thus I failed to try.

My friends would always say to me, "You must try! In life, you have to take chances. You will not always be successful, but you must move forward." Those who fulfilled their dreams did not accomplish their goals easily; they did not achieve success without some difficulty. Some had to overcome many obstacles. From this I learned that endurance leads to accomplishment. But I was often too laid-back, always looking for the easy way out.

I kept this attitude for many years, and it led to great disappointment. Now, in my senior years, I have decided to make some changes. I realize that, for many years, I was my own setback. Although it may seem late, I am now moving forward - better late than never!

Life offers many possibilities and changes along the way.

We've seen this with our own eyes in 2020. The year started out well, then changed drastically due to COVID-19. At first, we did not know how long the changes would last, but we now know that life will never be quite the same. Children have had to approach school in  new ways. While we pray they can cope, we can only imagine the impact these changes are having on their imagination and mental health.

Nonetheless, teachers and parents are working together to make the best of these changes and guide our young leaders of tomorrow toward great careers and bright futures.

Let's make the most of the changes that have taken place in our world. It's never too late to make a change in your life, to accomplish a goal, to adjust to your environment and find a path to success.

# Moving Forward

Think of the good old days, when one could go to school without breakfast, or even without a textbook. You would meet up with a friend at his home on your way to school, and his mom would offer you breakfast before you both took off. When you got to school, someone would share their textbook with you. People were more caring. You might have crossed paths with kids getting into a fist fight, but after some bruises and a couple of days, they were friends again. Those were happy days.

When I look around in these modern times, I feel sorry for the newer generations. Many of them are growing up in difficult circumstances, robbed of their childhood by no fault of their own, and are now adjusting to the effects of a global pandemic. Never in my lifetime have I seen something so devastating up close. Then, to make matters worse, the death of George Floyd - and countless others, sparked an uprising in the nation, adding to the heavy burden of the times.

We can all seek to move forward and make a change. Stay in school and receive a good education- your future lies in your bookbag. You can still become whoever you want to be. Believe in yourself, be respectful, and show concern to those in your community. Your generation can make a difference.

Your community will be proud as they see hope and leadership rising in you. They will see a generation moving forward to a brighter future.

# Stand Back

When we view our options in life, are we satisfied? Let's be honest with ourselves: life's struggles can be very overwhelming. The question that comes to mind is this- where or to whom can we turn? The answer may be surprising, but there is an inner voice in all of us that says, "You cannot fight the fight in your own strength; self has no power. There has to be another way."

In Scripture, we are reminded from where our help comes. At times, we must stand back, be led by divine counsel, and move by faith. Then, our approach - and our choices - will be different.

Most of us may have learned at an early age that life is full of ongoing struggles. But when we look back at history, it reminds us of the hardship and persecution our ancestors overcame in order to make the way clear for us to succeed, to get a good education and to think big. They were very courageous. They fought through blood, sweat and tears. We must carry on their legacy.

There are no limits to what you can do or what career you can choose. We can build better lives. Uphold the mantle, move forward to greater heights, and keep on striving to make this world a better place- one of trust, love and equality for all.

## About the Author

Joan Calliste loves the lord ,she has a passion for humanity, cares deeply about people especially those who are less fortunate,she motivates her readers to set goals dream big , have faith in God .she also loves traveling,shopping and spending time with family and friends.

www.ingramcontent.com/pod-product-compliance
Lightning Source LLC
Chambersburg PA
CBHW051245120626
46547CB00014B/1796